The Ferry Keeper

The Ferry Keeper

poems

Judith H. Montgomery

GRAYSON BOOKS
West Hartford, Connecticut
graysonbooks.com

The Ferry Keeper
copyright © 2024 by Judith H. Montgomery
published by Grayson Books
West Hartford, Connecticut
ISBN: 979-8-9888186-9-4

Book & Cover Design by Cindy Stewart
Cover Photo by https://unsplash.com/@ChristopherKuzman
Author Photo by Loretta Slepikas

For
William E. Howard
(1919–2015)
and
Jeanne C. Howard
(1920–2011)

Oh that it were in my power and that I had the strength
to bring you back to light from the dark of death
with oars on the sunken river.

—Euripides, *Alcestis*
(tr. Philip Vellacott)

Contents

The Ferry Keeper

becomes the only boat. Lays
her body flat, bellying black

water that licks below the dock.
Her chest a prow, her face the fixed

gaze of a figurehead. Steadied
against drift, she shivers as her pale

family clambers in. Stem and stern,
they shift from pain to place,

wanting not to spill across the bow.
Their crutches, tanks of oxygen,

prop stiff on her thwarts. Setting
match to wick and wax, her parents

light a candle to counter dark,
set it burning at her hull of bone,

while bearded medics fumble loose
the rope. Cast off, her boarders brace

their feet against the staves of her ribs,
arrange an offering of coins, an arc

of glitter about the shadowed candle.
Hot wax drips to sear the keel

that is her spine. Unmoored, she sets
course toward a compassless horizon.

Bearing her burdens on her back, she
strokes toward what she must believe

to be the other shore.

Where Light Collects

after a bedside photograph, dated 1943

For courtesy, they pause—mid-step in fox-trot—
    and ease their bodies one half-breath apart,
        but do not turn to look into the lens. The flash

has etched on paper his meticulously parted hair,
    lace ripple of her clinging dress. All else fades
        behind—crepe-paper sway, the other dancers'

stopped steps. So *proper*, this couple who
    carry within them the urge that will be me.
        Her bodice barely grazes his lapel. It's not

their bodies where the light collects. Light lives
    inside their gaze, a subtle current hum. They see
        only each other, even as daughters will be born,

and will try them. As her waist will thicken,
    his careful hair skimp gray. Her mind will clot
        and fail, until at last he must hail a bus to visit

his beloved who will not be certain of his name,
    though her eyes will glisten when he steps across
        the foster home's cane-worn sill. They'll settle

close on the couch, he tucking her inside
    the arc of his arm. She will doze on his arthritic
        shoulder, two fused one in October's gold slant.

I slip the image back in place, between glass
    and velvet backing. Here may they hover,
        oblivious to what waits beyond the flash.

Apprenticed

Early June, and my mother's four prize Peace roses shine
with a rare iridescence. Opulent satins—blush-pink, cream,

glistered green of ripe leaves—now doubly burnished
by a host of raiders brilliant in metallic blue-green head

and thorax, in copper-colored sheaths sheltering each wing.
The Japanese beetles glimmer in humid light as they eat

buds out from heart to skin, ravage each leaf down to skeleton.
Aghast at plunder, my mother sends my father out to slay

the invaders sapping her beloved shrubs. Rapt, I watch
as he tips the snouted canister of gas, decanting amber

poison to a jar to rid her world of pests. He spies the beetles'
hiding places, readies the death-trap, steadies it below.

Nudges the gorgeous bodies in. I fidget, eager for my turn
to serve. I learn how to clap lids tight, to keep the beetles

deep inside. Hold out my jam jar clogging with the lacquered
dead, my ears pink with praise. I learn how to sacrifice—

to make my mother smile. How beauty has its consequences.
Obligations. Price.

One Year Past My Wedding, My Mother and I

drive the Taconic toward White Plains. But someone's
tire tracks gouge the green verge, and traffic's stopped

in both lanes. We stop too—a man taps our window:
bad accident, driver rolled into the road. My mother

looks at me. *What should we* ... someone lies dead,
or bone-broken, bleeding. We grab a blanket, the car's

first-aid kit. Hurry toward the wreck, where three
others stand about the driver. We kneel beside him—

it's a young man—my wedding photographer.
My mother holds his hand, calls him back into life.

Reminds him of his name. I tuck the blanket by his ribs,
knees—his body's shaking into shock. I witness how

my mother mothers him. See what it is, will be, will
cost, to mother. Inside my body coils a sack of eggs

that will be my sons, sons for whom I will kneel
beside an icy soccer field, a gurney, clutching a hand

or banished to the ER waiting room. Compassion—
how we stumble into such accidental moments,

rise to meet another's suffering. For our own—
for anyone's son or daughter. Bound by blood

or heart, or not. Where two or three. Where one.

Crabapple *(Malus)*

Shorn of last year's extravagant display—
    pink-petalled snow on resurrecting grass
        below—the crabapple in my garden creaks

and shudders under February ice. I must
    trust that still the tree prepares for sap-rise,
        its hidden spread of roots and rootlets

to feed the emptied crown. Sometimes
    storm will expose the rootwad's grip
        when a crabapple's canopy topples under

winter—the tangled web a maze of stones
    and boulders thralled in subtle growth.
        As with my elder son. Just this morning,

his brain cancer's greedy branching—
    exposed by the scanner's penetrating beam.
        Oligodendroglioma: unrelenting tentacles

eel the winding tunnels. I know it's not
    malice. But I seethe as I watch my son lift
        his bone China cup of tea, talking of endurance.

The cankered growth grows. He awaits
    radiation. Hopes to reach April. May the tree's
        roots hold. Blossoms rise unblasted.

Still Speaking of Survival

Anticipating silence, I rank my tools—
    spade, trowel, secateurs, cultivator, bucket—

mute surgeon, advancing on the garden.
    Ready to set weed to right, to prepare

for the coming. But kneeling on the earth
    before a latticework of thorns, I strip aside

my gloves, thumb through loam and withered
    stems of last year's dried geranium—sift

white-fingered rootlets blindly spelling
    generation in a palm of upturned soil.

Despite the stiffening of late silver frost,
    the grass before my gaze will not be dumb,

but shifts in a murmuring of sun. Sprung
    maples whicker in the wind, buds constructing

a storm of double-winged seeds readying
    for flight, as light breaks open once again,

as pollen descends, a hail of yellow
    blessings on early slugs' scrawled glissade

of script. All morning I listen to earth
    speak of survival. The garden stirs and buzzes

in a spell of holy tongues, call-and-response
    spiriting a landscape bound by borders, but

limitless for increation—each voice loosed
   in verdant celebration—sign, signature, and stall:

   to chill. The winnowing. The fall.

What My Mother Has Left

behind—luxuriating beds of Peruvian lilies,
    alstroemeria, cream and amethyst petals
        testimony to her green heart. They bloomed

beneath the windows of the valley home
    my parents left to move close to me—
        high dry desert plateau where such lilies

fail to thrive, wincing at zero. Where
    my father unfolds her metal walker
        from the trunk and gently steers her

to the plastic tubs in Safeway. She points
    to a handful of rubber-banded blossoms—
        pale pink this week—and he fetches them,

will awkwardly array them in the green vase
    that anchors their assisted-living rooms.
        The new blooms yearn toward window sun,

and the leaves—twisting, leaning for light—
    pale to yellow as they age. When I knock,
        the door's little blue glass heart quivers

on its nail. My father opens to welcome
    me into their home, but before I can bend
        to kiss the off-kilter rouge roses on my mother's

cheek, or praise the new bouquet, she wails,
    "oh I've got alstroemeria," and I'm stopped
        short by her distress. "Alstroemeria," she says,

"my mother had it and it's catching up to me"—
she taps her forehead as though to dislodge
another stuck word. My father and I glance

above her head. We catch her twisting diction.

On The Comb as Outward and Visible Sign

Her white hair's been wind-ruffed—
    the way a dandelion's haloed globe
        drifts open—and when my mother

stops, four steps inside our home,
    my father stops behind her, and draws
        her comb, blue as the Virgin's cloak,

from his pocket. With exquisite
    care he redeems each blown strand
        into its proper curve, although

she does not know she's mussed or
    even that he combs, her arms already
        open to claim the hug she craves

from each of us—while the eager
    spaniel wreathes about our halted
        bodies, while my husband waits

to slip inside and shut the door
    behind. It's as though every atom
        in the room lights here, on the comb,

on my father's office of attendance—
    he who abandoned what he thought
        was a calling to the priesthood—

leaving off the white collar,
    shutting firmly behind him
        the brass-hinged seminary door

to step, bride glowing on his arm,
    into this other future of devotion.
        Vowing to make her life at last

perfect, and she perfectly loved.
    And here she stands, her hair
        gleaming, even while her mind

dims, as the ministering comb
    is raised and stroked and lowered,
        and our family stops,

lowering its head, to bow again
    before the contract, the blessing.

If

Oh, if the candle made of wax and wick—
the wick that links flame and candle flesh—

could light my mother's restless bed
and the tangled paths of her thought and sight—

If I could strike a red-tipped match against
the edges of my corrugated heart—

could marry the magic of wax and wick
to fire and bring the candle closer

to her wrinkled sheets, her chalky
wrinkled skin and her winding mind—

past the hoarded keeps of wrung tissues—
the wrappers of eucalyptus drops—

I would. I would. But my cardboard
heart is soaked with sweat and weeping.

I strike. Strike.

My Mother Stars in Her Own Grimm Fairy Tale

She fights her future. "I should never have been born.
You should never have been born." She must believe

some uninvited fairy has stitched deep inside her brain
an evil gift—genetic trick to be inherited by me.

Does she mean to relieve me of this dark award—not
to be nicked by the poisoned spindle? After lunch,

I open the apartment door to let her push the walker
back into the room, but she twists to fix me with her

ice gaze. "Who invited you in?" O interloper daughter.
Unwelcome guest. Alzheimer's thorny creep will keep

thicketing the palace of her world—soon she won't
know who she has become. But I remain the child

wished *never born*. Oh dear mother changeling—
who was it crept in from the dark woods to touch you,

warp you to another self, not the woman in the mirror
who asked only to be loved? Who'd guess how you'd

be trapped in your own fairy tale—withered crone, troll
beneath a bridge, both banished princess and wicked

queen stinging grief in each of us? *Should never have
been born.* Did you mean to spare me or condemn me?

The sharp spindle pricks. This wound won't heal.

Mother's Day at Aspen Ridge Assisted Living

My mother, decked out in gaudy sea-blue beads
saved from Mardi Gras last winter, will eat nothing

but a roast potato, two iced pastries, lifting each
with a blurred *who-are-you* air. My father cuts

her roasted chicken into tempting bites, but
she hungers only for sweets as she slips beneath

a whirlpool of *otherness*—too far out for me
to reach and pull her back to land, pat her dry,

fetch her tea, ask about abandoned knitting.
At diagnosis, she wept—she raged—when

they named it, what she'd most feared in life.
Now she drifts in some *dead-woman-float,*

listing on her back. Not knowing, no longer
caring how she's swept toward that foggy bank.

I can't tell whether to be glad for this small mercy,
or heart-struck-numb. Her doctors write a raft

of maybe-pills. None of these will keep her head
above the waves. I wipe my eyes. Can't bear

to watch across the tablecloth. Tides seep beneath
the door, rise above our knees. We hold her hands.

We try to remember how to wade back to shore.

Handed Her Remains

O, to hold your mother
in your hands! Clasp the knotted
box (ash: kiss: bone)—gone.

Tarnish

Oxygen's sly chemistry kisses silver
a darker shade. Little shining pig—

barely sketched in silver winged ears
and attentive snout—you have bathed

all year in air, yielding to tarnish.
I can run my thumb across your sleek

slopes—haunch and belly chilled
by winter's incursions at the sill.

Dear smirched sweet pig, you are no
magic lamp. No ghost figure can

return across the waters. But I cannot
watch you blotch above my desk.

Cool silver better mirrors sorrow.
I rub your curves. My fingertips

blacken. You shine like ice.

Snake, Shining

Waking from a restless flux of dreams,
I dress and step outdoors, into the stony

road's dazzling sun. Tree shadows shift
above the sloping stretch to the river,

pulsing as though alive—hiding, then
revealing a gleaming shape in darker shade.

Glory be to God for dappled things
slides like music through my head, though

this dappling is just an effect of light
and breeze that wanders the green layers

of leaves, summer shelter against sun.
I nudge the sleek body with my stick,

hoping he can slip away. He shines, but
does not move. The small head's crushed—

not quick enough to duck a truck's
ribbed tire. I've stopped because he's

been stopped, his suave S-curves still
ribboned in silver stripes. *Saving* isn't

up to me, or to the snake, whose busted
beauty I lament, how quickly quickness

has left him. If only I could step back-
wards into sun, reverse the scene.

Make the truck back away, the snake
plump up into life, flicker quick

into brush, safe in that shadow where
all of us must end.

My Father the Mathematician Has Fallen

again. The E.R.'s midnight pillow bleeds
fractals beneath his head. Pinned under

squares of sterile light, he shouts *DNR!*
DNR! from the gurney to an audience

of zero in his curtained cubicle. Breath
clots in my throat as they let me enter,

I can hardly speak my name. When he
understands who is with him, he tells me

what has happened as though it were
a story problem he has solved, despite

the sharp flash of pain and light as he fell
full-body backward to the tiled geometry

of the kitchen floor. How he remembered
to press the life-line on his wrist, how

the aides called the numbers, 9-1-1. But
he frets about the ambulance, the gurney,

the bother to the EMTs, not to mention
adding up the costs in his frugal head.

He seems not to be aware that his split
scalp still weeps blood, does not yet know

how this fall has jarred something loose
inside, concussion that in three months'

time will rob his tongue of words, numbers—
his equation-solving mind of answers

to what he knows must be simple problems.
For now he's intent on reminding anyone

in the room not to bring him back
if his heart stops, which it has not, not

yet, even as the reddened pillow signals
some essential loss. I won't remind him

later of what I hear pouring from his lips:
DNR: Do Not Resuscitate. He has long

since decided. He will *not* be a burden.

Driving after Dark

Late, I'm hurtling home in an aging frame
through pitch, headlights carving tunnels

out of black. Red eyes sting the road ahead,
warning of some coming buck and stop.

Monarch, Lignite, Butter Creek—inter-
sections where river teeth wait patient

for a slip. *Deer Crossing—Next 1 Mile ...*
what shadow smacked bloody on bumper

spurred the highway crew to mark these
sites? Then, like bones hung in the mirror

of the night, four crosses leap out white
as they ascend the slope from where I drive

until I'm to be spilled and stopped. Someone
nailed two sticks to form each cross,

scratched letters into paint. For miles, I catch
my blank face in the glass, writ over by

the white-eyed flare of crosses hovering
brighter than my dashboard lights. I brake.

Brake again. As though I could postpone
my exit through the crowded night.

My Father Takes a Shower

Or no: he is *given* one. He lowers his bones
    into the sturdy pale-green bath chair I brought
        last night. Its feet grip the slippery tiles.

He's guided by the pretty therapist, who
    will wash him, rinse him clean, wrap him
        in the soft cream-colored towel, while I wait

discreetly by the door. She'll make sure
    he doesn't fall and gash his scalp again,
        which would mean an ambulance, a fuss.

For now, this bliss of heated water to ease his fragile
    limbs, his nape, his belly and his privates, less
        private than before. He struggles upright, calls

on his manners to thank the helper who's about
    to give him the bad news: he can't do this
        by himself anymore. From now to the end

of his days, he'll have to be *assisted*. He'll wince
    and shrink from her professional assessment—
        woman who stands in for me, bossy daughter

with opinions he doesn't want to hear. Instead he
    will have to swallow her judgment, awful Gospel
        nudging him toward *helpless*, where he refuses

to go. "That's like someone sentenced to Hell,"
    he says, "no one ever comes back from *Assisted*."
        Tonight he'll set his walker by the wall. Take off

the thick smudged glasses. Fumble out his hearing
    aids, as she swaps the cannula puffing oxygen to
        his failing heart, lungs, brain. He'll let her peel away

the tan compression stockings before he swivels
    under sheets. Then, little will connect him to this
        world. Her verdict can't be heard. Only his pale

heart beating *No. Not yet. Not yet. Not yet.*

Linger

The Early Girl leans heavy on the bars
    of the cage. In October's slow cold,

two last tomatoes hang on. Half-red,
    half-yellow, they hug their seeds,

soak in late sun, huddle against fall.
    What else to do today but admit

to slippage, gather this last harvest?
    Then pause before the plant's

gnarled stem, its drying leaves,
    the green branch dangling two

persistent buds. Even to kneel
    and give thanks before this taking,

thanks before setting the grave
    shovel to the roots.

Moving My Father

Stippled, scarlet-lipped, the alstroemeria
        have worn out their water.
The vase clouds yellow as newborns

who slide into jaundice after birth, or
        the aged who loose
their grip on life, illness writ on skin.

At his tiny kitchen sink, I lift the bunch
        one-handed. Blackened
stems drip as I clip the necessary inch

from each slick stalk, dump the clotted
        water out. It pools above
the vortex of the drain. I run the tap, fill

the glass with water purified by rain
        and stone, I edge
the saved bouquet in, below the rim.

Wipe the glass, set vase and stained
        flowers back
on his table washed by pale November

light ... scarlet petals drop
        soundless, giving in to gravity.

First Night

My father's settled to sleep in his dim-lit
    room, quieted by water-murmur slipping
        down the hospice fountain. I can wander

now to the common room, where a vase
    of blue hydrangeas fills the dusk window.
        In a lit bookcase, a crowd of compact discs—

Mozart, Gershwin. Bach. Some say hearing
    is the last sense to go. My fingers light
        on the *Moonlight Sonata*—and I can see

my father bent above his mother's Baby
    Grand. A handful of discs, a CD player—
        I return with music to fill his failing body—

his hands too knotted now to touch
    any keys. Wanting to carry him on a skiff
        of sound across the slow lake of leaving,

I slide the *St John Passion* into the slot,
    to lift him and me out of body into Bach's
        grand flow. Beyond the window, dusk

deepens as I wait for the chorale to offer
    lull, *Ruht wohl*—*rest well*—so we may drift
        the certain and uncertain currents of this night.

Abide

Abide with me; fast falls the eventide …

The bedside phone breaches sleep, meaning time
    to pull on my discarded clothes, shiver on a coat,
        and set out in the car, headlights drawing me

on white threads through dank April chill, and despite
    my hurry, I feel as though I'm moving under water,
        entering *timelessness* as I slip through the door's

pale curtain pulled across for privacy, a world
    outside time, except what might be measured by
        pulse and breath, counted or not counted, number

that holds me here with my father, but in this room
    there is only *now*—even air suspends us, odor of
        peeled orange lingering as my own breath lingers—

as I enter vigil in which there is *before*, and to
    which there will be *after*, but for *now* we dwell,
        while beyond dark windows the tide of dew

arrives, rising as vapor, descending in endless
    cycle down to slough, stream, sea. I settle beside
        the last bed in which he will lie, breathing *until* …

the room drifts like a boat upon a still lake,
    my father faintly rocking in his bed, his pale skin,
        his flickering pulse—and I reach to touch his hands,

to hold him while I cling to the intimate buoy
    of his breath, for the balance of the night sending
        words his way, murmuring presence across his

slowing body, until at last he arrives—we arrive—
    at that final pulse in his throat. Now, *now* I'm
        called to count the seconds—sometimes those

dying will pause between breaths, pause longer,
    longer—which means nothing until time enters
        the room with that stopped breath, and the body

is released by whatever might be spirit rising
    into timelessness while I am clocked back
        into hours and days and years—marked,

    marked by *abide*, by rise and fetch of eventide ...

Notes

"The Ferry Keeper"

In Greek mythology, Charon is known as the ferry keeper of Hades. Charon took those who passed away on a journey across the rivers Styx and Acheron to reach the underworld. His fee for carrying the dead across the rivers to the underworld was a single coin. Charon was the son of Nyx, the Greek Goddess of Night, and of Erebus, Darkness.

"Crabapple *(Malus)*"

Malus is the genus name for the crabapple.
Oligodendroglioma is from the Greek: *oligo-* (few, little), *dendron* (tree), *glioma* (glue).

"Snake, Shining"

The italicized words are from Gerard Manley Hopkins' "Pied Beauty."

"Abide"

The epigraph is from an old hymn, *Abide with Me*, by Scottish Anglican cleric Henry Francis Lyte.

Acknowledgments

Grateful thanks to the editors and publishers who chose these poems, or earlier versions of them:

Cider Press Review: "The Ferry Keeper"

The Comstock Review: "Mother's Day at Aspen Ridge Assisted Living"

Cumberland River Review: "Apprenticed," "Where Light Collects" (as "Where the Light Collects"), "Snake, Shining," (as "Dead Snake")

Evansville Review: "Still Speaking of Survival (as "Speaking of Survival")

Evening Street Review: "My Father Takes a Shower," "Abide"

Forage Poetry: "What My Mother Has Left"

The Grief Diaries: "Handed Her Remains" (as "My Husband is Handed Her Remains")

Healing Muse: "My Father the Mathematician Falls," "Moving My Father"

High Desert Journal: "Driving after Dark"

The Inflectionist Review: "If"

Poetry Magazine: "Tarnish"

Quiet Diamonds (Orchard Street Press): "Linger" (as "Harvest")

Tar River Review: "Crabapple *(Malus)*"

Valparaiso Poetry Review: "On the Comb as Outward and Visible Sign," "One Year past My Wedding, My Mother and I Drive" (as "Where Two or Three")

"Driving after Dark" also appeared in the chapbook *Pulse and Constellation* (2006).

"On the Comb as Outward and Visible Sign" also appeared in *Litany for Wound and Bloom* (2018) and in the anthology *Storms of the Inland Sea: Poems of Alzheimer's and Dementia Caregiving* (2022).

"Mother's Day at Aspen Ridge Assisted Living" was nominated for a Pushcart Prize.

"What My Mother Has Left" and "Mother's Day at Aspen Ridge Assisted Living" also appear in *Poetry for the Dementia Journey* (2024).

~

I hold close to my heart these wonderful poets and supporters:

With grateful thanks, first, to Ginny Connors of Grayson Books, and to B. Fulton Jennes, poet laureate emerita of Ridgefield, Connecticut, for selecting this book and bringing it into being. Additional thanks go to Cindy Stewart for her elegant design work on the book.

For inspiration, friendship, and scintillating critiques of my poems, I am ever indebted to Paulann Petersen, Andrea Hollander, Cindy Williams Gutierrez, Diane Holland, Dianne Stepp, Margaret J. Chula, Donna Prinzmetal, Christine Delea, Penelope Scambly Schott, John Morrison, Gerry Foote, Frances Adler, Mike Langtry, Stephanie Striffler, Daniel Hobbs, Emily Ransdell, Pamela Crow, Patricia Bolin and Carol Barrett.

Very special thanks to the keen-eyed readers of *The Ferry Keeper* in manuscript, Dianne Stepp and John Morrison, and to my mentors of many years, Maxine Scates and Andrea Hollander, who press me onward when I most need it.

For the double loan of their beach cottage for retreat into words and silence during the making of this chapbook, a deep bow to Frank and Nancy Weintraub.

Enduring thanks to the support of Literary Arts over the years, as well as to the Oregon Cultural Trust. Both entities make wonderful art blossom.

And my grateful heart always to all my family for their warm interest in and support of my life and work, especially to my husband Phil.

About the Author

Judith H. Montgomery cared for her mother and father in their declining years, as well as for her husband in his cancer journey (see *Mercy*). *The Ferry Keeper* chronicles her care for, and sometimes frustrations with, her parents on their final journey. Montgomery's poems appear in *Poet Lore*, *Gyroscope*, and *Tahoma Literary Review*, among other journals, as well as in a number of anthologies. She's been awarded fellowships in poetry from Literary Arts and the Oregon Arts Commission; residencies from Playa, Hypatia-in-the-Woods, and Caldera; and prizes from the *Bellingham Review*, *Persimmon Tree*, and elsewhere. Her first chapbook, *Passion*, received the 2000 Oregon Book Award for Poetry. *Red Jess*, a finalist for several national first book prizes, appeared in 2006. Her second full-length book, *Litany for Wound and Bloom*, was a finalist for the Marsh Hawk Prize, and appeared from Uttered Chaos Press in 2018. *Mercy*, which received the Wolf Ridge Press Narrative/Poetic Medicine Chapbook award, appeared in 2019. This chapbook, *The Ferry Keeper*, was also a finalist for the Comstock Poetry Chapbook competition. She holds a PhD in American Literature from Syracuse University, and loves to talk about making and revising poems.

www.ingramcontent.com/pod-product-compliance
Lightning Source LLC
Chambersburg PA
CBHW060357130626
46553CB00003B/1271